Microsoft
Power Automate

The Microsoft 365 Companion Series

Dr. Patrick Jones

OLYMPUS ACADEMY
PRESS

TABLE OF CONTENTS

STREAMLINING YOUR WORKFLOW

In a world where efficiency is key, every minute counts. Repetitive tasks, manual processes, and scattered workflows can drain time and energy, leaving less room for the creativity and strategic thinking that drive real success. Microsoft Power Automate offers a solution—a tool designed to automate your day-to-day tasks, optimize processes, and give you back what matters most: time.

Imagine a tool that connects your apps, organizes your data, and executes tasks on your behalf—all without requiring advanced coding skills. That's the promise of Power Automate. Whether you're a professional looking to streamline your workflow, a small business owner trying to manage tasks efficiently, or a curious learner eager to explore automation, Power Automate is your gateway to working smarter, not harder.

Automation isn't just for tech experts anymore. Microsoft Power Automate makes automation accessible to everyone, from beginners to seasoned pros. Its intuitive design empowers users to create workflows—known as "flows"—that connect apps, services, and data across the Microsoft ecosystem and beyond.

For example:

- **Send automated email reminders:** Never miss a deadline again.
- **Organize files effortlessly:** Automatically save email attachments to SharePoint or OneDrive.
- **Monitor your business in real-time:** Receive notifications when key metrics hit a certain threshold.

Power Automate doesn't just simplify work; it transforms it.

1

This book is your comprehensive guide to mastering Microsoft Power Automate. Through step-by-step instructions, practical examples, and relatable stories, you'll learn how to:

- Understand what Power Automate is and why it's a game-changer.

- Get started with creating simple flows and exploring the interface.

- Implement best practices for building efficient and reliable workflows.

- Unlock advanced features like approvals, conditional logic, and data integration.

- Discover tips and tricks to save time, troubleshoot issues, and enhance your skills.

- Integrate Power Automate with Microsoft 365 tools like Teams, Outlook, and SharePoint.

- Learn how AI-powered Copilot can assist you in designing workflows with ease.

- Avoid common pitfalls that can slow down or disrupt automation projects.

Throughout this book, you'll follow Sarah, a team leader overwhelmed by recurring tasks and fragmented processes. Initially skeptical of automation, she discovers the power of Power Automate to streamline her daily responsibilities. From managing approvals to organizing data, Sarah's story highlights the transformative potential of automation and shows how you can apply these lessons in your own workflow.

Written in a conversational, approachable style, this book demystifies Power Automate's features, making even the most advanced tools feel accessible. It's designed for anyone eager to embrace automation—no technical expertise required. Whether you're automating simple tasks or building complex workflows, this guide will empower you to make the most of Power Automate.

The journey to mastering Power Automate begins here. By the end of this book, you'll not only understand how to use this powerful tool but also feel confident in applying it to your unique needs. Get ready to save time, increase productivity, and unlock new possibilities. Let's dive into the world of automation and transform the way you work!

WHAT IS MICROSOFT POWER AUTOMATE?

Imagine a tool that works tirelessly in the background, taking care of repetitive tasks, connecting your apps, and simplifying processes—all so you can focus on what matters most. That's Microsoft Power Automate. It's not just an automation tool; it's a productivity powerhouse designed to streamline workflows, improve efficiency, and make technology work for you.

Power Automate allows you to create workflows—called "flows"—that automate tasks across apps, services, and data. These workflows can be as simple as sending a daily email reminder or as complex as managing multi-step business processes. With Power Automate, automation is no longer limited to developers and IT professionals; it's accessible to everyone, from beginners to experts.

At its core, Microsoft Power Automate is a cloud-based platform that connects various applications and services. These connections enable automation of tasks, the transfer of data, and the creation of streamlined processes.

Let's look at the key components that make up Power Automate:

1. **Flows:**
   A flow is the heart of Power Automate. Think of it as a step-by-step sequence of actions that automate a specific task or process. Flows can range from simple (e.g., sending an email when a file is uploaded to OneDrive) to complex (e.g., managing an approval process across multiple teams).

2. **Triggers:**
   Every flow starts with a trigger, which is an event that sets the flow into motion. Triggers can be manual (e.g., pressing a button) or automatic (e.g., receiving an email).

3. **Actions:**
   Actions are the steps that follow a trigger. For example, if the trigger is receiving an email, an action might be saving the email attachment to a folder in OneDrive or notifying a team in Microsoft Teams.

4. **Connectors:**
   Power Automate supports hundreds of connectors, allowing you to link apps and services. These include Microsoft 365 tools like Teams, Outlook, and SharePoint, as well as third-party apps like Slack, Dropbox, and Twitter.

5. **Templates:**
   Not sure where to start? Power Automate offers a library of pre-built templates for common workflows, such as sending notifications, copying files, or tracking tasks.

Power Automate operates on a simple principle: trigger, action, result. Here's how it typically works:

1. **Define the Trigger:**
   Identify the event that will start the workflow. For example, a new file uploaded to a folder in OneDrive.

2. **Set Actions:**
   Determine what happens next. For the OneDrive example, the action could be notifying a team in Teams or emailing a link to a colleague.

3. **Execute and Monitor:**
   Once the flow is active, Power Automate handles the task whenever the trigger occurs. You can monitor flows in real-time and make adjustments as needed.

Example: Sarah created a flow to automatically save email attachments from her inbox to a SharePoint folder. Every time she receives a report, the flow triggers, saving her hours of manual work each week.

Why is Power Automate Unique?

1. **No Coding Required:**
   You don't need to be a developer to create powerful workflows. Power Automate's drag-and-drop interface and intuitive design make it accessible to everyone.

2. **Integration Across Platforms:**
   Power Automate seamlessly connects Microsoft 365 tools with third-party apps, enabling cross-platform workflows.

3. **Flexibility and Scalability:**
   Whether you're automating personal tasks or managing enterprise-level processes, Power Automate scales to fit your needs.

4. **Cloud-Based Efficiency:**
   As a cloud-based tool, Power Automate is always on, ensuring your workflows run smoothly, no matter where you are.

Power Automate is versatile, with applications in various settings:

- **In the Workplace:** Automate routine tasks, manage approvals, and connect teams.

- **For Small Businesses:** Simplify customer interactions, streamline operations, and track data.

- **In Education:** Manage schedules, send reminders, and organize materials.

- **For Personal Use:** Track expenses, set reminders, or organize digital files.

Example: A small business owner uses Power Automate to automatically gather customer inquiries from their website and organize them into a SharePoint list, ensuring no lead is overlooked.

Power Automate isn't just a standalone tool; it's deeply integrated into the Microsoft 365 ecosystem. This allows it to connect with apps like Teams, Excel, and SharePoint, as well as external services.

- **With Teams:** Automate notifications, update team channels, or schedule messages.
- **With Excel:** Extract, organize, and share data effortlessly.
- **With SharePoint:** Manage files, track updates, and streamline approvals.

Pro Tip: Combine Power Automate with Microsoft AI features, like Copilot, to build smarter, more adaptive workflows.

In today's fast-paced world, automation isn't a luxury—it's a necessity. Power Automate empowers you to take control of your workflows, eliminate redundancies, and focus on tasks that require creativity and critical thinking.

Whether you're an individual looking to simplify your daily tasks or an organization seeking to optimize operations, Power Automate is the tool that bridges the gap between technology and productivity.

Now that you understand what Power Automate is, it's time to explore why it's such a valuable tool.

WHY USE MICROSOFT POWER AUTOMATE?

Imagine a world where repetitive tasks are completed without lifting a finger, where processes run seamlessly in the background, and where your focus shifts to more meaningful work. Microsoft Power Automate makes this vision a reality. By automating workflows and connecting tools, Power Automate allows you to reclaim your time, boost productivity, and collaborate with ease.

This chapter explores the key reasons why Power Automate is an essential tool for individuals, teams, and businesses alike. Whether you're looking to save time, reduce errors, or foster collaboration, Power Automate has something valuable to offer.

1. Save Time and Eliminate Repetitive Tasks

Why It Matters:
Repetitive tasks like data entry, email follow-ups, or file organization can consume a significant portion of your day, leaving less time for strategic thinking or creative work.

How Power Automate Helps:

- Automates routine processes, like saving email attachments to SharePoint or updating spreadsheets.

- Schedules recurring tasks, such as sending weekly reports or reminders.

- Runs workflows in the background, freeing you to focus on what matters most.

Example: Sarah, a project manager, created a flow to automatically generate task reminders for her team every Monday morning. This saved her the hassle of manually sending emails and ensured her team stayed on track.

2. Reduce Human Errors

Why It Matters:
Manual processes are prone to errors, whether it's forgetting to send an email, misplacing data, or overlooking a deadline. These mistakes can disrupt workflows and create unnecessary stress.

How Power Automate Helps:

- Ensures consistency by executing tasks exactly as programmed.

- Reduces the risk of human error in data entry, file organization, and communication.

- Tracks workflows in real-time, making it easy to identify and correct issues.

Example: A small business owner used Power Automate to automatically generate invoices and send them to clients, eliminating errors caused by manual entry.

3. Enhance Collaboration

Why It Matters:
Modern work requires seamless collaboration, especially in remote or hybrid environments. Without the right tools, team communication can become fragmented and inefficient.

How Power Automate Helps:

- Sends automated notifications to Microsoft Teams channels when files are updated or tasks are completed.

- Integrates with SharePoint to ensure teams have real-time access to the latest documents.

- Streamlines approval processes, ensuring quick and transparent decision-making.

Example: Sarah used Power Automate to notify her team in Teams whenever a new file was uploaded to their shared SharePoint folder, keeping everyone aligned and informed.

4. Improve Productivity and Efficiency

Why It Matters:
Time wasted on low-value tasks adds up, impacting overall productivity. Power Automate optimizes workflows, ensuring you can do more in less time.

How Power Automate Helps:

- Combines multiple steps into a single workflow, eliminating manual intervention.

- Enables task prioritization by automating non-critical activities.

- Supports integration with AI tools, like Copilot, to enhance decision-making and workflow design.

Example: Sarah used Power Automate to extract data from her team's reports and compile them into a single spreadsheet, saving hours of manual work each week.

5. Bridge Gaps Between Tools and Systems

Why It Matters:
In a world where businesses rely on numerous apps and platforms, disconnected systems can slow down workflows and hinder productivity.

How Power Automate Helps:

- Connects Microsoft 365 apps with third-party tools like Dropbox, Salesforce, or Slack.

- Transfers data seamlessly between systems, ensuring continuity and reducing redundancy.

- Integrates with over 500 connectors to create unified workflows.

Example: Sarah connected Power Automate to her CRM and email, ensuring that every new customer inquiry was logged automatically and a follow-up email was sent instantly.

6. Foster Scalability and Adaptability

Why It Matters:
As your needs grow, so do the demands on your workflows. Manually scaling processes can be time-consuming and unsustainable.

How Power Automate Helps:

- Scales workflows to handle larger volumes of data or users without additional effort.

- Adapts to changing requirements with customizable templates and easy-to-edit flows.

- Integrates with AI-driven features to make workflows smarter over time.

Example: Sarah started with a simple flow to organize her files but later expanded it to handle team-wide task assignments, proving that Power Automate could grow with her needs.

7. Empower Non-Technical Users

Why It Matters:
Automation shouldn't be reserved for IT experts. Power Automate democratizes automation, making it accessible to anyone, regardless of their technical expertise.

How Power Automate Helps:

- Offers an intuitive, drag-and-drop interface for designing workflows.

- Provides pre-built templates to simplify common processes.

- Offers guided tutorials and resources to help users get started quickly.

Example: Sarah, who had no prior coding experience, built a flow to automate her approval requests using one of Power Automate's templates, saving her hours of manual work.

8. Leverage AI for Smarter Workflows

Why It Matters:
AI-powered tools like Copilot enhance automation by introducing intelligent decision-making and predictive capabilities.

How Power Automate Helps:

- Uses AI to analyze data and suggest workflow improvements.

- Allows Copilot to assist in building and optimizing workflows.

- Automates complex tasks, such as sentiment analysis or language translation.

Example: Sarah used Copilot to design a flow that prioritized customer support tickets based on sentiment analysis, ensuring urgent issues were addressed first.

Microsoft Power Automate is more than a tool; it's a gateway to transformation. By saving time, reducing errors, and improving collaboration, it empowers users to focus on what truly matters.

GETTING STARTED WITH MICROSOFT POWER AUTOMATE

Starting your journey with Microsoft Power Automate can feel both exciting and a bit overwhelming. With its vast potential for automation, the possibilities may seem endless. But don't worry—this chapter is your step-by-step guide to getting started. By the end, you'll have the confidence to create your first flow and explore how Power Automate can transform your tasks and workflows.

1. Setting Up Power Automate

Before diving into flows, ensure you're ready to use Power Automate.

- **Accessing Power Automate:**
  Power Automate is included with most Microsoft 365 subscriptions. You can access it through:

  - The Microsoft 365 app launcher (waffle menu) by selecting Power Automate.

  - Directly via flow.microsoft.com.

- **Sign In:**
  Use your Microsoft 365 account credentials to log in. Once signed in, you'll land on the Power Automate dashboard.

Example: Sarah opened Power Automate through her Microsoft Teams app to integrate automated notifications into her project workflows.

2. Exploring the Power Automate Interface

The dashboard is your control center for creating and managing flows. Here's a quick tour:

- **Home Tab:** View suggested templates, tutorials, and popular flows.

- **My Flows:** Manage your existing flows, see their status, and edit or delete them.

- **Templates:** Access pre-built templates to jumpstart your automation journey.

- **Create:** Start from scratch or use guided steps to design a new flow.

Pro Tip: Spend a few minutes exploring the dashboard to familiarize yourself with its layout.

3. Creating Your First Flow

Let's walk through creating a simple automated flow. Imagine you want to save all email attachments you receive into a specific OneDrive folder.

Step-by-Step Guide:

1. **Go to the Dashboard:** Click Create to start building a new flow.

2. **Choose Flow Type:** Select Automated Cloud Flow (starts when a trigger occurs).

3. **Set a Trigger:**
   - In the search bar, type Outlook and select When a new email arrives.
   - Define conditions (e.g., only apply to emails with attachments).

4. **Add an Action:**
   - Search for OneDrive and choose Save attachment.
   - Select the OneDrive folder where attachments will be saved.

5. **Save and Test:** Click Save, then send a test email to ensure the flow works as expected.

Example: Sarah used this flow to automatically organize client reports into specific folders, saving her time every week.

4. Using Templates to Save Time

Not sure where to start? Power Automate offers a vast library of templates for common tasks:

- **Examples:**
  - Notify a Teams channel when a new file is added to SharePoint.
  - Send a daily email with a summary of your calendar.
  - Track Twitter mentions of your brand in an Excel sheet.

How to Use Templates:

1. Navigate to the Templates section on the dashboard.
2. Search for a specific task or browse by category.
3. Select a template and customize it to fit your needs.

Example: Sarah used a pre-built template to track tasks in Planner and notify her team when due dates approached.

5. Testing and Monitoring Your Flows

Once your flow is active, it's essential to ensure it works correctly:

- **Testing:** Use the Test button to simulate the flow and verify its functionality.
- **Monitoring:** Check the status of your flows under My Flows. You can see whether they ran successfully or encountered errors.

- **Troubleshooting:** If a flow fails, Power Automate provides error messages and suggestions for fixes.

Pro Tip: Start with simple flows to build your confidence before tackling more complex workflows.

6. Leveraging Connectors for More Powerful Flows

Connectors are the backbone of Power Automate, enabling integration between different apps and services.

- **Popular Connectors:**
  - Microsoft 365 tools like Outlook, SharePoint, and Teams.
  - Third-party apps like Salesforce, Dropbox, and Google Drive.
  - Social media platforms like Twitter and LinkedIn.

How to Add Connectors:

1. Search for the app you want to connect in the flow editor.
2. Select the connector and authorize access.

Example: Sarah linked her CRM software to Power Automate, automatically adding new leads to an Excel sheet for easy tracking.

7. Exploring Advanced Options

Once you're comfortable with basic flows, explore advanced features to expand your automation capabilities:

- **Conditional Logic:** Create branches in your workflow based on specific conditions.
- **Approvals:** Use Power Automate to streamline approval processes, such as vacation requests or expense reports.

- **AI Builder:** Integrate AI models to analyze data, detect objects in images, or extract text from documents.

Example: Sarah used conditional logic to send task reminders only to team members who hadn't completed their assignments by a specific date.

8. Best Practices for New Users

To ensure a smooth start with Power Automate, follow these tips:

- **Start Small:** Begin with simple flows to understand the basics.
- **Use Templates:** Don't reinvent the wheel—start with pre-built workflows.
- **Test Frequently:** Regularly test your flows to identify and resolve issues early.
- **Ask for Help:** Leverage Power Automate's community forums and support resources for guidance.

Getting started with Power Automate is just the beginning. With a solid understanding of its interface and features, you're ready to dive deeper into best practices, tips, and tricks for creating efficient and impactful workflows.

BEST PRACTICES FOR MICROSOFT POWER AUTOMATE

Creating workflows with Microsoft Power Automate can simplify tasks, save time, and boost productivity. But like any tool, its effectiveness depends on how you use it. In this chapter, we'll explore best practices to help you design efficient, reliable, and scalable flows that maximize the power of automation.

1. Start Small and Build Gradually

Why It Matters:
It's tempting to dive into complex workflows right away, but starting small allows you to master the basics and gain confidence.

Best Practices:

- Begin with single-step flows, such as saving email attachments to OneDrive or sending an automated reminder.

- Gradually add complexity, introducing conditions, multiple actions, or loops as you become more comfortable.

- Use templates as a foundation and customize them to fit your needs.

Example: Sarah's first flow organized her team's documents into SharePoint folders. As she gained experience, she expanded it to include notifications and approvals.

2. Plan Your Workflow Before Building

Why It Matters:
Rushing into flow creation can lead to inefficiencies, errors, or redundant steps. Planning ensures clarity and purpose.

Best Practices:

- Outline the steps of your workflow on paper or using a flowchart tool.

- Identify triggers, actions, and outcomes before you start building.

- Map out edge cases, such as what happens if data is missing or an action fails.

Example: Before automating her team's task management process, Sarah sketched a flow diagram to visualize each step, avoiding unnecessary complications.

3. Use Descriptive Names and Comments

Why It Matters:
As you create more flows, keeping them organized becomes crucial. Descriptive names and comments make your workflows easier to understand and maintain.

Best Practices:

- Name your flows clearly, reflecting their purpose (e.g., "Weekly Report Reminder" or "Customer Onboarding Workflow").

- Add comments within the flow editor to explain complex steps or logic.

- Use consistent naming conventions for variables and actions.

Example: Sarah renamed her flow from "Flow 1" to "Marketing File Organizer," making it easier to identify in her dashboard.

4. Test Frequently and Monitor Performance

Why It Matters:
Testing ensures your flows work as intended and helps you identify issues early. Regular monitoring prevents disruptions.

Best Practices:

- Test your flow after creating each step to verify functionality.

- Use the Power Automate dashboard to monitor flow performance and success rates.

- Enable notifications for flow failures and review error messages promptly.

Example: Sarah tested her task notification flow by simulating various scenarios, catching an issue with date formatting before it affected her team.

5. Optimize for Efficiency

Why It Matters:
Efficient flows save time and resources, ensuring faster execution and better reliability.

Best Practices:

- Minimize unnecessary steps or redundant actions.

- Use batch processing when handling large volumes of data.

- Leverage conditional logic to execute actions only when needed.

Example: Sarah optimized her data transfer flow by combining multiple actions into a single batch operation, reducing processing time by 50%.

6. Leverage Triggers Effectively

Why It Matters:
Triggers define when and how a flow starts, so choosing the right one is essential for accuracy and timeliness.

Best Practices:

- Use specific triggers, such as "When a file is created in a folder," rather than broad ones.

- Set trigger conditions to avoid unnecessary executions (e.g., only trigger when an email is marked urgent).

- Consider using manual triggers for workflows that don't require automation every time.

Example: Sarah used a manual trigger for her client summary flow, ensuring it only ran when she was ready to share the report.

7. Use Variables and Dynamic Content Wisely

Why It Matters:
Variables and dynamic content enable personalization and flexibility in your flows, but improper use can lead to errors or confusion.

Best Practices:

- Define variables early in the flow to keep steps organized.

- Use dynamic content sparingly to avoid overcomplicating actions.

- Test variable values during execution to ensure accuracy.

Example: Sarah used dynamic content to personalize task reminders with each team member's name, making her notifications more engaging.

8. Secure Your Flows

Why It Matters:
Flows often handle sensitive data, so ensuring security is critical.

Best Practices:

- Limit permissions for shared flows to prevent unauthorized access.

- Use environment variables to separate sensitive data from the flow logic.

- Regularly audit your flows for potential security risks.

Example: Sarah added role-based access controls to her approval flow, ensuring only managers could review and approve requests.

9. Take Advantage of Copilot

Why It Matters:
Copilot's AI-powered assistance can simplify flow creation and optimize workflows.

Best Practices:

- Use Copilot to suggest actions and conditions for complex workflows.

- Ask Copilot to review your flow for potential inefficiencies or improvements.

- Leverage Copilot for troubleshooting by asking, "Why did this flow fail?"

Example: When building a multi-step workflow, Sarah asked Copilot for suggestions to streamline her approval process, saving her significant time.

10. Regularly Review and Update Your Flows

Why It Matters:
Business needs and software updates change over time. Regularly reviewing your flows ensures they remain relevant and effective.

Best Practices:

- Schedule periodic reviews to evaluate flow performance and relevance.

- Update outdated connectors or triggers as needed.

- Incorporate new Power Automate features to enhance functionality.

Example: Sarah reviewed her client onboarding flow quarterly, updating it to reflect changes in her company's processes.

By following these best practices, you'll create flows that are efficient, reliable, and adaptable to your needs.

TIPS AND TRICKS FOR MICROSOFT POWER AUTOMATE

Microsoft Power Automate is a versatile tool with a wide range of features designed to make your workflows seamless and efficient. While its core functionalities are user-friendly, there are many lesser-known tips and tricks that can significantly enhance your experience. In this chapter, we'll dive into practical shortcuts, advanced techniques, and hidden features to help you unlock the full potential of Power Automate.

1. Clone Flows to Save Time

Why It's Helpful:
If you frequently create similar workflows, cloning existing flows can save you the effort of starting from scratch.

Tricks:

- Open your flow and click on Save As to duplicate it.

- Modify the cloned flow to fit your new requirements.

Example: Sarah cloned her "Weekly Report Reminder" flow to create a "Monthly Metrics Notification" flow, adjusting only the timing and data sources.

2. Explore the Power of Nested Conditions

Why It's Helpful:
Complex workflows often require decisions based on multiple conditions. Nested conditions allow for more dynamic and adaptable flows.

Tricks:

- Use "Condition" actions to branch workflows based on multiple criteria.

- Combine conditions with logical operators like AND and OR for greater precision.

Example: Sarah set up a flow to notify her manager only if an invoice was overdue and exceeded a certain amount, reducing unnecessary alerts.

3. Take Advantage of Advanced Expressions

Why It's Helpful:
Expressions in Power Automate allow you to manipulate data, perform calculations, or dynamically set values in your flows.

Tricks:

- Use the concat() function to combine text strings.

- Apply the formatDateTime() function to standardize dates in your workflows.

- Leverage if() statements for conditional logic within a single step.

Example: Sarah used the formatDateTime() function to ensure all her task deadlines were displayed in the same format across multiple apps.

4. Automate Approvals with Ease

Why It's Helpful:
Power Automate's approval workflows streamline decision-making processes, keeping everyone on the same page.

Tricks:

- Use the Start and Wait for an Approval action to notify approvers and track their responses.

- Customize approval emails to include relevant details and action buttons.

- Send reminders automatically if an approval is delayed.

Example: Sarah created an approval flow for her team's expense requests, ensuring all submissions were reviewed and approved without delays.

5. Utilize Copilot for Workflow Optimization

Why It's Helpful:
Copilot, Power Automate's AI-powered assistant, simplifies the process of building, optimizing, and troubleshooting flows.

Tricks:

- Ask Copilot to suggest actions or connectors based on your goals.
- Use Copilot to identify inefficiencies and recommend improvements.
- Prompt Copilot to troubleshoot failed flows and provide actionable fixes.

Example: Sarah used Copilot to streamline a multi-step flow by combining redundant actions, improving its execution time significantly.

6. Schedule Flows for Optimal Timing

Why It's Helpful:
Scheduling flows ensures tasks are executed at the right time, improving efficiency and preventing disruptions.

Tricks:

- Use the Recurrence trigger to schedule flows at specific intervals (daily, weekly, monthly).
- Combine scheduling with conditions to execute flows only when necessary.

Example: Sarah scheduled her team's task summary emails to be sent every Monday morning, aligning perfectly with their weekly planning meetings.

7. Integrate Third-Party Connectors

Why It's Helpful:
Expanding your workflows beyond the Microsoft ecosystem allows you to connect with popular third-party apps.

Tricks:

- Use the Dropbox connector to back up files automatically.

- Integrate Salesforce to log new leads and update customer data.

- Connect Twitter to monitor mentions and engage with your audience.

Example: Sarah linked her company's Twitter account to Power Automate, ensuring every brand mention was logged in Excel for social media analysis.

8. Debug and Troubleshoot with Run History

Why It's Helpful:
Run history provides detailed logs of your flows, making it easier to identify and fix issues.

Tricks:

- Check run history to view a step-by-step execution of your flow.

- Use error details to pinpoint failed actions and correct them.

- Test individual steps to isolate problems without affecting the entire workflow.

Example: When a flow failed to send notifications, Sarah reviewed the run history and found that a connector had expired, resolving the issue in minutes.

9. Use Environment Variables for Flexibility

Why It's Helpful:
Environment variables allow you to define reusable settings, making your flows adaptable across different scenarios.

Tricks:

- Store API keys, URLs, or default values as environment variables.
- Update variables without editing the flow logic.

Example: Sarah used environment variables to manage different email templates for her team's notifications, making updates quick and effortless.

10. Archive Old Flows

Why It's Helpful:
As your needs evolve, archiving outdated flows keeps your workspace organized and prevents confusion.

Tricks:

- Export unused flows as .zip files and store them for future reference.
- Disable flows instead of deleting them to retain their logic.

Example: Sarah archived an old approval flow when her company switched to a new process, preserving her work in case it was needed again.

Power Automate's versatility lies in its combination of simplicity and depth. By applying these tips and tricks, you can create workflows that not only meet your current needs but also adapt to new challenges.

REVOLUTIONIZING WORKFLOW AUTOMATION

Microsoft Power Automate is already a powerful tool for streamlining tasks and automating workflows. With the integration of Copilot, Microsoft's AI-powered assistant, Power Automate enters a new realm of efficiency and innovation. Copilot transforms the way workflows are built, optimized, and managed, making automation more accessible and effective for users of all experience levels.

In this chapter, we'll explore how Copilot integrates seamlessly with Power Automate, helping you design smarter workflows, solve challenges, and unlock the full potential of automation.

Copilot is an AI assistant designed to enhance your Power Automate experience. It acts as a partner in creating, refining, and troubleshooting workflows, using natural language processing to understand your goals and offer intelligent suggestions.

Think of Copilot as a collaborator who simplifies complex processes and eliminates the guesswork in automation. Whether you're a beginner looking to create your first flow or an advanced user tackling intricate workflows, Copilot is there to guide you every step of the way.

How Copilot Enhances Power Automate

1. **Simplifies Workflow Creation**

   o   With Copilot, you can describe what you want to automate in plain language, and it will suggest a starting point.

   o   For example, you can type, "I want to save email attachments to SharePoint," and Copilot will create a basic flow for you to refine.

Example: Sarah needed a flow to notify her team in Teams when a file was uploaded to SharePoint. By typing her requirements, Copilot suggested a template and pre-configured the steps, saving her hours of manual setup.

2. **Optimizes Existing Flows**

   o Copilot can analyze your workflows and recommend ways to streamline them.

   o It identifies redundant steps, inefficient actions, or missing logic, offering solutions to improve performance.

Example: Sarah's approval flow had several unnecessary conditions slowing it down. Copilot suggested merging conditions, cutting execution time by 30%.

3. **Troubleshoots Issues**

   o When a flow fails, Copilot provides detailed explanations of the error and actionable fixes.

   o Instead of manually diagnosing issues, you can ask Copilot, "Why did this step fail?"

Example: Sarah's notification flow stopped working due to an expired connector. Copilot identified the issue and walked her through reconnecting the service.

4. **Suggests Advanced Features**

   o For users looking to expand their skills, Copilot introduces advanced Power Automate features like conditional logic, loops, and custom connectors.

   o It also recommends relevant templates, triggers, and actions based on your workflow.

Example: Sarah wanted to add sentiment analysis to her customer feedback flow but wasn't sure how. Copilot suggested integrating AI Builder and guided her through the setup.

Using Copilot in Power Automate

Here's how to get started with Copilot:

1. **Enable Copilot:**

   o Copilot is built into Power Automate, accessible from the flow editor or dashboard.

   o If you don't see it, ensure your environment supports Copilot and that it's enabled in your Microsoft 365 settings.

2. **Ask for Assistance:**

   o Use the Copilot interface to type natural language prompts, such as:

      ▪ "Create a flow that sends reminders for overdue tasks."

      ▪ "Optimize this flow to reduce execution time."

      ▪ "What connectors can I use to integrate Salesforce with Teams?"

3. **Refine and Test:**

   o Review Copilot's suggestions and make adjustments to align with your goals.

   o Test the flow to ensure it meets your requirements.

Best Practices for Using Copilot

1. **Be Specific:**

- The more detailed your prompts, the better Copilot can tailor its suggestions.
- Instead of saying, "Create a flow," specify, "Create a flow that emails me when a file is added to OneDrive."

2. **Iterate and Experiment:**
   - Don't hesitate to refine Copilot's suggestions or ask for alternative approaches.
   - Use Copilot as a starting point and build on its ideas.

3. **Combine Features:**
   - Pair Copilot's insights with Power Automate's testing and monitoring tools for maximum effectiveness.

4. **Leverage Learning Opportunities:**
   - Pay attention to how Copilot structures flows and incorporates advanced features—it's a great way to learn new techniques.

Real-World Applications of Copilot in Power Automate

1. **Small Business Efficiency:**
   - A small business owner uses Copilot to automate customer inquiries, ensuring every question is logged in a CRM and followed up with an email.

2. **Education Management:**
   - A school administrator creates flows to manage student attendance notifications and schedules using Copilot's guidance.

3. **Enterprise Operations:**

o   A large organization uses Copilot to optimize multi-department approval workflows, reducing processing time by half.

Example: Sarah's team integrated Copilot-powered workflows to track project milestones across departments, improving communication and accountability.

Challenges and How Copilot Overcomes Them

- **Complex Workflows:** Copilot simplifies intricate workflows by breaking them into manageable steps.

- **Knowledge Gaps:** For users unfamiliar with advanced features, Copilot provides explanations and suggestions.

- **Flow Failures:** Copilot's troubleshooting capabilities ensure issues are resolved quickly.

Copilot takes Power Automate to the next level by combining AI-driven intelligence with user-friendly automation. As you continue your journey, remember that Copilot is there to support you, whether you're creating your first flow or mastering advanced workflows.

COMMON PITFALLS AND HOW TO AVOID THEM

Microsoft Power Automate is a robust tool for automating tasks and improving workflows, but like any technology, it's not without its challenges. Many users encounter common pitfalls that can lead to frustration, inefficiency, or even outright failure of their workflows. In this chapter, we'll explore these challenges and, more importantly, how to avoid or resolve them.

1. Overcomplicating Workflows

The Pitfall:
New users often try to pack too much functionality into a single flow, resulting in complexity that's hard to manage and troubleshoot.

Why It Happens:
The excitement of automation can lead to overly ambitious projects, especially when users attempt to automate multiple tasks at once.

How to Avoid It:
- Start small with simple, single-task flows.
- Break complex workflows into smaller, modular flows that interact with each other.
- Use templates as a starting point and gradually customize them.

Example: Sarah initially tried to create a flow that combined task notifications, file organization, and approval requests. By splitting it into three separate flows, she simplified the process and made troubleshooting easier.

2. Using Broad Triggers

The Pitfall:
Triggers that are too generic can cause flows to activate unnecessarily, leading to unintended outcomes or excessive executions.

Why It Happens:
Users may select a trigger like "When a file is created" without specifying a folder or file type, causing the flow to run for every new file in a large system.

How to Avoid It:

- Define specific triggers with clear parameters (e.g., a particular folder or file name pattern).

- Use conditions to filter events before actions are executed.

Example: Sarah refined her file upload notification flow by limiting the trigger to a specific project folder, reducing noise and improving relevance.

3. Ignoring Error Handling

The Pitfall:
Flows that lack error handling can fail silently, leaving users unaware of issues until they cause significant disruptions.

Why It Happens:
Error handling requires additional setup, which new users may overlook or deem unnecessary.

How to Avoid It:

- Include error-handling steps like retries or notifications for failed actions.

- Use the Configure Run After option to define what happens when a step fails.

- Regularly review the run history to identify and resolve issues.

Example: Sarah added a fallback action to her approval flow, ensuring that if an approver didn't respond within 24 hours, the request escalated to a backup approver.

4. Forgetting to Test and Monitor Flows

The Pitfall:
Skipping testing or monitoring can lead to flows that don't work as intended or stop functioning due to changes in connected services.

Why It Happens:
Users may assume a flow will work perfectly once created and fail to revisit it over time.

How to Avoid It:

- Test each step of your flow during creation and before deploying it.
- Enable notifications for flow failures and regularly check run history.
- Periodically review and update flows to ensure compatibility with system changes.

Example: Sarah tested her customer follow-up flow with a sample email before rolling it out to her entire team, catching a typo in the email template.

5. Overlooking Connectors and Permissions

The Pitfall:
Flows can fail if the connectors used lack proper permissions or if access to required services is revoked.

Why It Happens:
Users may not verify permissions during flow creation or forget to update them after changes in accounts or systems.

How to Avoid It:

- Ensure all connectors have the necessary permissions during setup.

- Use service accounts for connectors to avoid disruptions caused by individual account changes.

- Regularly audit connectors for expired tokens or missing access rights.

Example: When Sarah's company migrated email accounts, she updated her Outlook connector to prevent interruptions in her email-triggered workflows.

6. Failing to Document Flows

The Pitfall:
Without proper documentation, it can be difficult to understand, maintain, or hand off workflows, especially in collaborative environments.

Why It Happens:
Users may not see the immediate value in documenting flows or assume they'll remember how they work.

How to Avoid It:

- Add descriptive names and comments to every step in your flows.

- Maintain a central document or spreadsheet detailing the purpose, triggers, actions, and owners of each flow.

Example: Sarah created a shared spreadsheet for her team, outlining each flow's functionality and ownership, ensuring smooth transitions during team changes.

7. Overuse of Loops and Conditions

The Pitfall:
Excessive use of loops or complex conditions can slow down flows or even cause execution limits to be reached.

Why It Happens:
Loops and conditions are powerful but can lead to inefficiencies if not carefully implemented.

How to Avoid It:

- Optimize loops by batching actions where possible.

- Use filters and conditions to minimize unnecessary iterations.

- Monitor flow performance and adjust steps as needed.

Example: Sarah replaced a loop that processed individual tasks with a batch operation, significantly reducing execution time.

8. Not Leveraging Advanced Features

The Pitfall:
Relying solely on basic actions can limit a flow's potential and create inefficiencies.

Why It Happens:
Users may not explore advanced options like expressions, environment variables, or custom connectors.

How to Avoid It:

- Take advantage of Power Automate's extensive documentation and tutorials to learn about advanced features.

- Experiment with expressions to streamline actions and add logic.

- Use environment variables to simplify flow customization and management.

Example: Sarah used the concat() expression to dynamically generate email subject lines, adding clarity and personalization to her notifications.

By being aware of these common pitfalls and following the strategies outlined in this chapter, you can avoid unnecessary frustration and ensure your workflows remain efficient, reliable, and scalable.

SARAH'S AUTOMATION ADVENTURE

The soft hum of Sarah's laptop filled her quiet home office as she sipped her morning coffee, preparing for another busy day as a team leader. Her inbox was already bursting with unread emails, task notifications from various apps were piling up, and she had a list of repetitive tasks to tackle before her team meeting.

Sarah had heard about Microsoft Power Automate in passing but had never taken the time to explore it. Today, feeling overwhelmed by the chaos, she decided it was time to give automation a try.

Opening Power Automate for the first time, Sarah was greeted by its clean dashboard and a banner advertising pre-built templates. The idea of automating her tedious tasks sounded promising, but she didn't know where to begin.

Scrolling through the templates, one caught her eye: "Save email attachments to OneDrive." Every week, her team emailed her project reports that she manually downloaded and organized into folders. With a glimmer of hope, Sarah clicked the template and began customizing it.

With just a few clicks, she set up a flow that saved all email attachments tagged with "Weekly Report" to a specific folder in her OneDrive. After testing it with a sample email, she watched in awe as the flow worked flawlessly.

"That's one less thing to worry about," she thought with a smile.

Buoyed by her initial success, Sarah decided to tackle a more complex workflow: notifying her team in Microsoft Teams whenever a new file was added to their SharePoint folder. This task had become a source of frustration, as her team often missed updates and fell behind on projects.

She began building the flow step by step, selecting SharePoint as the trigger and Teams as the action. When configuring the notifications, Sarah realized she wanted to include the file name and a link for easy access. Feeling stuck, she noticed the Copilot icon in the corner and decided to give it a try.

"Can you help me add a link to the file in the Teams notification?" she typed into Copilot.

Within seconds, Copilot suggested the perfect solution, adding the necessary dynamic content to her flow. Testing it with a dummy file upload, Sarah was thrilled to see the notification appear in her team's channel, complete with the file link.

"This will save so much time and confusion," she thought, marveling at the simplicity of it all.

Not everything went smoothly, though. Sarah's next project involved automating an approval process for her team's expense requests. She built the flow confidently, adding an approval trigger and configuring it to send emails to the managers responsible for approvals.

But when she tested the flow, it failed to execute properly. The approval emails weren't being sent, and she couldn't figure out why. Frustrated but determined, Sarah opened the flow's run history.

The logs pointed to a permissions issue with the email connector. Remembering a tip from the Power Automate documentation, she adjusted the connector's settings to use her team's shared service account instead of her personal account. After re-testing the flow, everything worked perfectly.

"This could have been a disaster if I hadn't checked the run history," she realized, grateful for the lesson learned.

Over the next few weeks, Sarah became a Power Automate enthusiast. She automated a variety of tasks, from organizing team calendars to managing feedback surveys. Each new flow freed up time and mental energy, allowing her to focus on leading her team more effectively.

She even started exploring advanced features like conditional logic and batch processing, with Copilot guiding her through the more complex setups. The once-daunting world of automation had become her ally, transforming the way she approached work.

During a team meeting, Sarah shared her newfound passion for Power Automate, demonstrating a few of her workflows. Her colleagues were amazed by the possibilities and eager to try automation for themselves.

"Think about the time we can save and the stress we can avoid," Sarah encouraged. "With tools like Power Automate, we can work smarter, not harder."

Sarah's story is a testament to the power of automation and the impact it can have on productivity, collaboration, and peace of mind. What tasks in your day-to-day life could Power Automate simplify?

POWER AUTOMATE AND YOUR JOURNEY

As we conclude this exploration of Microsoft Power Automate, it's clear that automation isn't just about simplifying tasks—it's about transforming how you work, think, and collaborate. Throughout this book, we've delved into the many facets of Power Automate, from understanding its features to creating workflows that save time and reduce errors. Let's revisit the key takeaways and reflect on how Sarah's story illustrates the potential for transformation in your own journey.

A Recap of Power Automate's Power

1. **What is Power Automate?**
   At its core, Power Automate is a tool that connects apps, automates tasks, and streamlines workflows. It empowers users to create "flows" that handle everything from sending notifications to managing complex approval processes, all with minimal effort.

2. **Why Use Power Automate?**
   By automating repetitive tasks, reducing errors, and fostering collaboration, Power Automate frees up your time and energy for what truly matters. It's a tool for anyone seeking to improve productivity and efficiency in their personal or professional life.

3. **Getting Started and Building Confidence**
   From simple templates to advanced flows, Power Automate offers an accessible starting point for all users. By mastering the basics and gradually exploring its deeper features, you can design workflows that adapt to your unique needs.

4. **Best Practices and Tips**
   The best workflows are well-planned, efficient, and secure. Using descriptive names, testing frequently, and leveraging Copilot's

AI-powered guidance can ensure your flows are reliable and impactful.

5. **Avoiding Pitfalls**

   While challenges like complex workflows or insufficient permissions can arise, they're easily managed with the right strategies. Power Automate's run history, error-handling options, and community support are invaluable resources for troubleshooting and improvement.

6. **The Role of Copilot**

   Copilot takes Power Automate to the next level, simplifying flow creation, optimizing performance, and resolving issues with ease. It's like having an automation expert at your side, ready to assist whenever needed.

Sarah's journey with Power Automate mirrors the potential for transformation in your own workflow. Let's reflect on her experiences:

- **Starting Small, Dreaming Big:**
  Sarah began with simple flows, like saving email attachments to OneDrive, and gradually tackled more complex challenges. This approach allowed her to build confidence and master the basics—a strategy that's just as effective for anyone new to automation.

- **Overcoming Challenges:**
  Sarah's story wasn't without its hurdles. From permissions issues to overly broad triggers, she encountered common pitfalls but learned to navigate them with tools like run history and Copilot. Her persistence highlights the importance of embracing challenges as opportunities for growth.

- **Transforming Productivity:**
  Through automation, Sarah freed herself from repetitive tasks, improved team communication, and enhanced her workflow

efficiency. Her success demonstrates how Power Automate can create space for meaningful, strategic work.

- **Sharing Knowledge:**
  By introducing her team to Power Automate, Sarah amplified its impact, fostering collaboration and inspiring others to explore automation. Her journey reflects the ripple effect of embracing technology and sharing its benefits.

Your journey may not look exactly like Sarah's, but the principles remain the same: start small, stay curious, and let automation work for you.

This book is just the beginning. Power Automate is part of a larger Microsoft 365 ecosystem, offering endless opportunities to integrate tools, optimize processes, and achieve your goals. Whether you're exploring Teams, SharePoint, or Copilot, the skills you've gained here will serve as a foundation for future growth.

As technology evolves, so do the possibilities for innovation and efficiency. By continuing to learn and experiment, you'll not only transform your workflows but also inspire others to do the same.

Like Sarah, you have the tools and potential to create meaningful change in your work and life. The key is to take that first step—whether it's automating a simple task or diving into advanced features.

EMBRACING THE POWER OF AUTOMATION

As we reach the end of this journey through Microsoft Power Automate, it's important to step back and reflect on what you've learned and how you can apply it to your own work and life. Automation is more than a convenience—it's a shift in how we approach tasks, collaborate, and innovate. Power Automate opens the door to a world where technology does the heavy lifting, giving you the freedom to focus on creativity, strategy, and growth.

Power Automate is more than a tool; it's a mindset. By automating repetitive tasks and streamlining workflows, you're not just saving time—you're reshaping how you work. This transformation goes beyond individual tasks and extends into team dynamics, organizational efficiency, and even personal growth.

Automation:

- **Frees up mental bandwidth:** Spend less time on mundane tasks and more on solving complex problems or innovating new ideas.

- **Enhances collaboration:** Create workflows that connect people, tools, and data, ensuring seamless communication and coordination.

- **Drives inclusivity:** Tools like Copilot make automation accessible to everyone, regardless of technical expertise, democratizing productivity gains.

Power Automate is a stepping stone toward building smarter, more connected systems that adapt to your needs and goals.

While Power Automate is a powerful standalone tool, its integration with the Microsoft 365 ecosystem takes its capabilities to another level. Imagine:

- Using Teams for real-time collaboration while Power Automate keeps the notifications flowing.

- Syncing SharePoint libraries with automated task assignments.

- Leveraging Copilot across apps to make your workflows even more intuitive.

Every Microsoft 365 app complements Power Automate, creating a synergy that multiplies your productivity. This book is just one chapter in understanding that ecosystem—other tools like Teams, SharePoint, and Word offer their own unique contributions to your workflow.

As you close this book, remember that learning is a continuous process. Power Automate, like any technology, is constantly evolving with new features and capabilities. Staying curious and engaged will help you stay ahead, whether it's exploring advanced features like AI Builder or discovering new ways to integrate third-party apps.

Here are a few steps to keep growing:

- **Experiment Regularly:** Try new workflows and features to expand your skills.

- **Engage with the Community:** The Power Automate user community is a wealth of knowledge and inspiration.

- **Explore Related Tools:** Other Microsoft 365 apps, like Power BI and Power Apps, offer complementary solutions for analytics and custom app development.

Your learning journey doesn't end here—it's just beginning.

This book is part of the Microsoft 365 Companion Series, designed to guide you through the tools that shape the modern workplace. From mastering OneDrive and Teams to exploring Copilot's AI-powered capabilities, each book offers practical insights and relatable stories to empower you on your journey.

By continuing to explore these resources, you'll build a toolkit that transforms how you work and connects you with the possibilities of the future.

Think back to Sarah's journey. Her story began with a few small steps: automating simple tasks, overcoming challenges, and sharing her successes with her team. Along the way, she transformed not only her workflows but also her mindset.

Your story can be just as transformative. Power Automate isn't just a tool for today—it's a gateway to tomorrow. It empowers you to adapt, innovate, and thrive in an ever-changing world.

So take what you've learned here, embrace the potential of automation, and continue exploring. The future of work is automated, connected, and exciting—and with Power Automate, you're ready to lead the way.

Thank you for joining this journey. Now, go out there and create workflows that inspire change and unlock your potential!